Sports Illustrated KIDS

BASEBALL'S Most CONTROVERSIAL PLAYS

YOU MAKE the CALL!

by Matt Chandler

CAPSTONE PRESS
a capstone imprint

Published by Capstone Press, an imprint of Capstone
1710 Roe Crest Drive, North Mankato, Minnesota 56003
capstonepub.com

Library of Congress Cataloging-in-Publication Data
is available on the Library of Congress website.
ISBN: 9798875257452 (hardcover)
ISBN: 9798875257407 (paperback)
ISBN: 9798875257414 (ebook PDF)

Summary: Dig deeper into three controversial baseball plays. The umpires made their calls, for better or worse. Now it's your turn to make the call.

Editorial Credits
Editor: Christianne Jones; Designer: Tracy Davies; Media Researcher: Svetlana Zhurkin; Production Specialist: Whitney Shaefer

Image Credits
Associated Press: John Minchillo, 11, Kathy Willens, 12, Mark Lennihan, 13, Paul Sancya, 21, Ron Frehm, 16; Getty Images: Adam Hunger, 29, Bettmann, 27, Chris Coduto, 10, Dylan Buell, 7, Jamie Sabau, 5, Justin Edmonds, 8, Patrick Smith, 6, Simon Bruty, 14, 15; Newscom: Icon SMI/Steven King, 19, imageBROKER/Jim West, 9, KRT/File, 25, ZUMApress/Detroit Free Press/Kirthmon F. Dozier, 20; Shutterstock: Eugene Onischenko, cover (bottom), Lana Sham, back cover, 17, 23, 28, 29 (right), Muhammad Muhdi (dotted background), cover (top) and throughout

Words in **BOLD** can be found in the glossary.

Printed and bound in China. PO 6459

TABLE OF CONTENTS

GAME-CHANGING CALLS

Imagine doing a job while thousands of people watch you in person. Millions more watch on television. If you get it wrong, social media will explode. Your failure could even spread around the globe.

Umpires make thousands of calls each season. A few milliseconds can be the difference between safe and out. Today, instant replay is used in Major League Baseball (MLB). It can help correct an umpire's bad call. Before instant replay, a bad call could completely change a game. It could **alter** a team's season.

IT COULD EVEN CHANGE THE OUTCOME OF THE WORLD SERIES!

As you read these stories of missed calls and blown plays, you'll get the chance to put yourself in the ump's shoes.

HOW WOULD YOU HANDLE THE PRESSURE? WOULD YOU MAKE A DIFFERENT CALL?

CHAPTER 1

THE IMPORTANCE OF UMPIRES

Umpires have a very hard job. They may make hundreds of correct calls each season. But fans only seem to remember the ones they get wrong.

There are two types of umpires on a baseball field. The home plate umpire calls balls and strikes. He also calls runners safe or out on scoring chances. The base umpires call runners safe or out at the bases. They also judge if a player makes a catch or if certain rules have been broken.

In Major League Baseball, there are four umpires used for each game. One for each base and one for home plate. In the playoffs, two umpires are added to work the foul lines in the outfield.

TIME OUT

In the minor leagues, two or three umpires are used. In Little League, it can vary between one and two umps.

It takes incredible skill and years of training to be a major league umpire. Many umps begin by working Little League or high school games. To become a professional umpire, they attend a five-week umpire school. The best may get the chance to umpire in college and semipro ball. The best of those can try out to umpire in the minor leagues.

THE FEW WHO MAKE IT TO THE MINORS FACE AN EVEN LONGER ROAD TO THE MAJOR LEAGUES.

There are only 76 full-time umpires in the majors. That means new chances don't open very often. When they do, hundreds of umpires apply to get a chance. Umpires attend training camps and audition for a chance to call games at the professional level.

TIME OUT

Umpires often work for years in the minors for very low pay just to get a shot at the big leagues.

Major League Baseball began using instant replay in 2008 to review home runs. It was **expanded** to cover other plays in 2014. Instant replay gives umpires the chance to correct a missed call. Managers can call for one review of a play per game.

Also, the head umpire can call for a review. If they determine a call is wrong, it can be fixed in real time. If the call is reversed, the manager gets to keep his review to use again if needed.

An umpire can only view a play at full speed. That's when technology comes in. It combines super slow motion with lots of camera angles.

IN THE MAJORS, THERE ARE AT LEAST 24 DIFFERENT CAMERAS CAPTURING EVERY PLAY!

TIME OUT

Fans watching at home see a white box on the screen that shows the strike zone. Each pitch is marked and shows every time the ump misses a strike call.

CHAPTER 2

HELPING JETER HOMER

The roar of the crowd at Yankee Stadium was deafening. It was Game 1 of the 1996 American League Championship Series. The New York Yankees were hosting the Baltimore Orioles. The Yankees were trailing 4–3 late in the game. That's when shortstop Derek Jeter walked up to the plate. He slapped the second pitch he saw deep to right field.

Outfielder Tony Tarasco drifted back to make the catch at the wall. Just as he reached up, a fan with a glove reached over the wall. The fan knocked the ball into the stands.

IS THAT A HOME RUN OR FAN INTERFERENCE?

UMPIRE RICHIE GARCIA SIGNALED A HOME RUN!

Orioles' manager Davey Johnson demanded the play be **overturned**. Garcia **ejected** Johnson from the game. His call stood. The Yankees won the game. They went on to win the club's 23rd World Series.

Replay clearly showed that the fan interfered. Garcia blew the call, but the play was allowed to stand.

The umpire admitted he got the call wrong after the game.

"Do I feel bad? Absolutely," Garcia said. Still, he said he doesn't believe he cost Baltimore the game. "I still feel he (Tarasco) wouldn't have caught that ball."

If Garcia had correctly ruled fan **interference**, he had options. He could have ruled that Tarasco would have caught the ball. Jeter would have been out. If Garcia believed Tarasco would not have made the catch, he could have awarded Jeter a double.

THERE IS NO WAY TO TELL HOW THE GAME WOULD HAVE ENDED.

You've been called in to replace **veteran** umpire Richie Garcia in right field.

Jeter steps up to the plate and hits a bomb. Tarasco jumps up to make the catch. A fan reaches out at the same time. You have a split-second to decide.

Is it a home run or fan interference?

If it is fan interference, you have a second call to make. Do you call Jeter out, or do you award him a double?

CHAPTER 3

THE ALMOST PERFECT GAME

On June 2, 2010, Detroit Tigers starter Armando Galarraga was one out away from pitching a perfect game against Cleveland. Then, in a split second, a blown call plunged Galarraga from perfection into heartbreak.

There were two outs in the top of the ninth inning. Galarraga had faced 26 batters. He had **retired** them all. Not a single hit, walk, or error. Then, Galarraga faced Cleveland's shortstop, Jason Donald. The pitcher let the ball fly, and Donald **chopped** it to the right side.

TIME OUT

In more than 150 years, only 24 MLB pitchers have thrown a perfect game.

Wilson

Tigers first baseman, Miguel Cabrera, raced to grab the ball. Galarraga sprinted toward first to cover the base. Cabrera hit his pitcher with a perfect throw as Galarraga's foot touched the bag.

RUNNER OUT. PERFECT GAME SECURED!

Except first-base umpire Jim Joyce called Donald safe! He broke up the perfect game! Tigers manager Jim Leyland argued the call. But Joyce stood by his ruling.

Incredibly, there was a bright side to one of the biggest blown calls in MLB history. Both men responded to the mistake with **noble** acts of sportsmanship. Immediately after the game, Joyce choked up as he apologized for missing the call.

"It was the biggest call of my career, and I kicked it," Joyce said. "I just cost that kid a perfect game."

Galarraga almost immediately defended Joyce, saying people make mistakes. He met with the umpire after the game, hugging him and later saying, "We're all human."

TIME OUT

Galarraga's "perfect game" is in the National Baseball Hall of Fame in Cooperstown. The Hall has a display featuring Galarraga's spikes along with the first-base bag from the game.

You are the first-base umpire.

Jason Donald hits the ball. Miguel Cabrera fields it.

Cabrera throws it to Armando Galarraga, who catches it and touches first base just as Donald runs over the base.

Was the runner safe or out? The play was incredibly close, and you have to make the call immediately.

CHAPTER 4

A ROYAL ROBBERY

The St. Louis Cardinals were three outs away from capturing the 1985 World Series. Pinch hitter Jorge Orta led off the bottom of the ninth inning by chopping a ball to the right side. Cardinals first baseman Jack Clark grabbed the ball and tossed it to **reliever** Todd Worrell, who was covering first.

Orta raced down the line at a blistering speed. He crossed the bag at the same time the ball was landing in Worrell's glove.

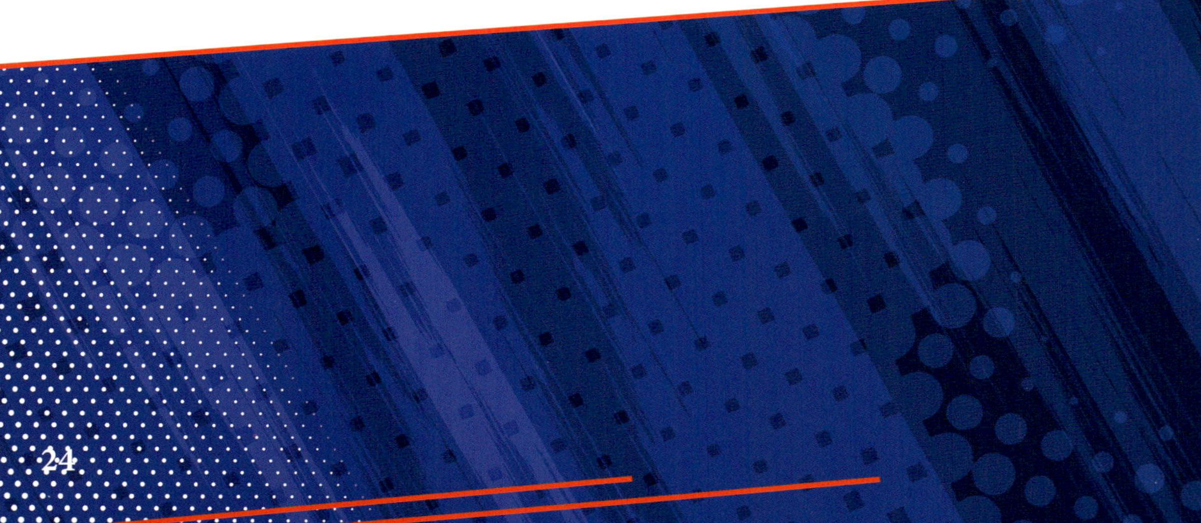

WHAT WAS THE CALL? WAS ORTA SAFE OR OUT?

SAFE, ACCORDING TO FIRST-BASE UMPIRE DON DENKINGER.

Replays from three different angles showed that Orta was out by a half step. Denkinger missed the call, but no amount of arguing would help. The Royals won the game on a walk-off hit. They went on to win Game 7 and bring the World Series trophy back to Kansas City.

Like the Galarraga call, this play involved a pitcher covering first base and taking a throw. In baseball, these are referred to as "bang bang plays." There is a lot of action, and it happens very fast. Watching the play at full speed, it is impossible to say Orta is out.

TIME OUT

In 2014, Denkinger said, "I just know that if the same thing happened now, they'd get it right on replay and it'd be over with."

This call did not directly cost the Cardinals the game. After the call, Clark misplayed a pop up that would have been an out. The Cardinals also had a passed ball error. Still, their fans see it as the World Series that was stolen from them.

It's your big shot as first-base umpire.

Jorge Orta hits the ball toward first base. Jack Clark grabs it and tosses it to Todd Worrell.

Worrell hits the base close to Orta stepping on it.

Was the runner safe or out? You get one chance to make the right call.

It's the World Series, and every call matters.

Being an umpire is a tough job. Most of the time they make the right call. But fans only remember the calls they miss. The next time you are watching a game, pretend you are the ump. Make the calls along with them. See how you do. If you play baseball, pay attention to how fast the game moves. Watch how many close calls there are.

Do you think you have what it takes to be a major league umpire someday?

COULD YOU MAKE THE CALL?

GLOSSARY

alter (AWL-ter)—to modify or change

chop (CHOP)—to hit into the ground, giving the ball a high bounce

eject (ih-JEKT)—to throw or toss out

expand (ik-SPAND)—to make bigger

interference (in-ter-FEER-uhns)—getting in the way or creating difficulties for someone

noble (NOB-buhl)—kind and positive

overturn (oh-ver-TURN)—to reverse or change

reliever (ri-LEE-ver)—a pitcher who enters the game after the starting pitcher has been removed

retire (ri-TAHY-uhr)—to put out a batter or base runner

veteran (VE-tuh-ruhn)—a person with lots of experience in a job

READ MORE

Berglund, Bruce. *Baseball GOATs: The Greatest Athletes of All Time*. North Mankato, MN: Capstone Press, 2022.

Buckley, James, Jr. *A Kids' Guide to the National Baseball Hall of Fame: The Greatest Players from Hank Aaron to Derek Jeter to Cy Young*. Bellevue, WA: Becker & Mayer! Kids, 2024.

Chandler, Matt. *Baseball's Origin Story*. North Mankato, MN: Capstone Press, 2025.

INTERNET SITES

National Baseball Hall of Fame
baseballhall.org

Sports Illustrated Kids: Baseball
sikids.com/baseball

Umpire Bible: Getting Started Umpiring
umpirebible.com/index.php/17-ump-info/71-getting-started-umpiring

INDEX

ABOUT THE AUTHOR

Matt Chandler is the author of more than 90 books for children and thousands of articles published in newspapers and magazines. He writes mostly nonfiction books with a focus on sports, ghosts and haunted places, and graphic novels. Matt lives in New York.